piano · vocal · guitar

TODAY'S HITS FOR WEDDINGS

ISBN 978-1-4584-1643-8

HAL•LEONARD®
CORPORATION

7777 W. BLUEMOUND RD. P.O. BOX 13819 MILWAUKEE, WI 53213

Visit Hal Leonard Online at
www.halleonard.com

BEFORE YOUR LOVE

Words and Music by GARY BURR,
DESMOND CHILD and CATHY DENNIS

Slow Ballad

I won-der how __ I ev-er made __ it through __ a day. __

How did I set-tle for a world __
All of my dreams __ seemed like cas-

in shades __ of gray? __
-tles in __ the sky. __

When you go __ in cir-cles, all __ the scen-
I stand be-fore __ you and __ my heart

Recorded a half step higher.

BLESS THE BROKEN ROAD

Words and Music by MARCUS HUMMON,
BOBBY BOYD and JEFF HANNA

D.S. al Coda

-ken road _____ that led me straight ____

to you.

EVERYTHING

Words and Music by AMY FOSTER-GILLIES,
MICHAEL BUBLÉ and ALAN CHANG

GOD GAVE ME YOU

Words and Music by
DAVE BARNES

To Coda ⊕

here — left to say. It's true: _____

God gave me you. _____

God gave me you. __

HALO

Words and Music by BEYONCÉ KNOWLES,
RYAN TEDDER and EVAN BOGART

Moderately

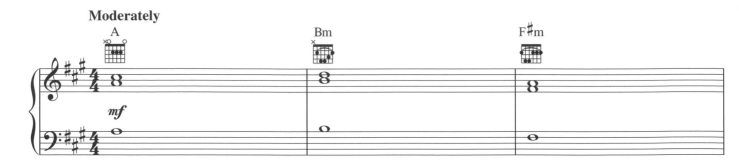

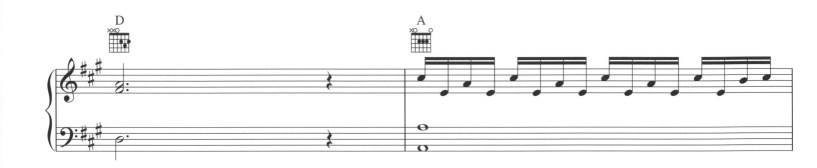

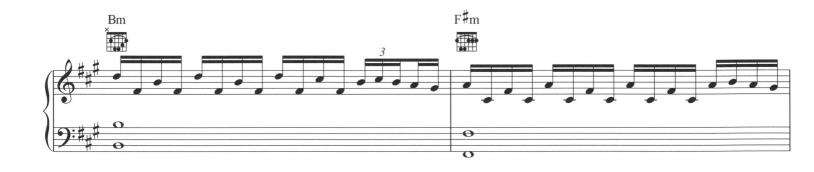

Re-mem-ber those walls I built?

* *Verse one is written an octave higher than sung.*

*Lead vocal sung both times at written pitch.

Vocal ad lib.

D.S. al Coda
(take 2nd ending)

Ev - 'ry-where I'm look - in' now, _

CODA

HERE

Words and Music by STEVE ROBSON
and JEFFREY STEELE

Moderately

I DO

Words and Music by COLBIE CAILLAT
and TOBY GAD

JUST THE WAY YOU ARE

Words and Music by BRUNO MARS,
ARI LEVINE, PHILIP LAWRENCE,
KHARI CAIN and KHALIL WALTON

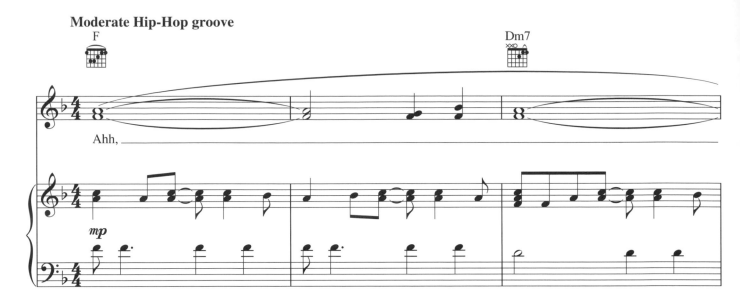

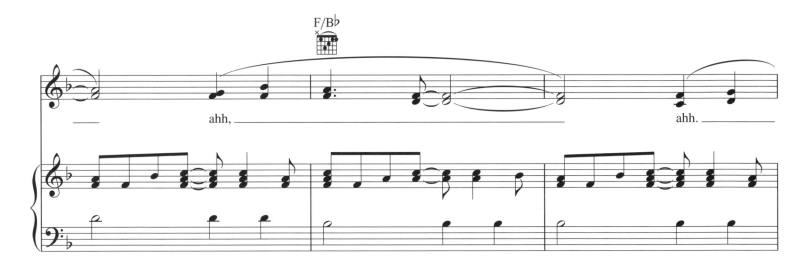

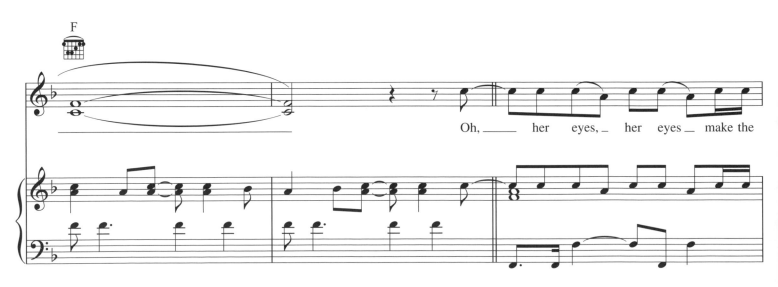

But ev-'ry time _ she asks _ me, "Do ___ I look _ o - kay?" _ I ___ say: ___

When I see your face, ___ there's not a thing ___ that I ___ would change, _

___ 'cause you're a - maz - ing _____ just ___ the way _ you are.

___ And when you smile, ___

LOVING YOU IS EASY

Words and Music by
SARAH McLACHLAN

LOVE STORY

Words and Music by
TAYLOR SWIFT

Moderately

We were both young when

I first saw ___ you. I close my eyes ___ and the flash-back starts. ___ I'm stand-in'

LUCKY

Words and Music by JASON MRAZ,
COLBIE CAILLAT and TIMOTHY FAGAN

*Substitute half rest on D.S.

MAKING MEMORIES OF US

Words and Music by
RODNEY CROWELL

MARRY ME

Words and Music by
PAT MONAHAN

MAMA'S SONG

Words and Music by LUKE LAIRD,
KARA DioGUARDI, MARTI FREDERIKSEN
and CARRIE UNDERWOOD

MINE

Words and Music by
TAYLOR SWIFT

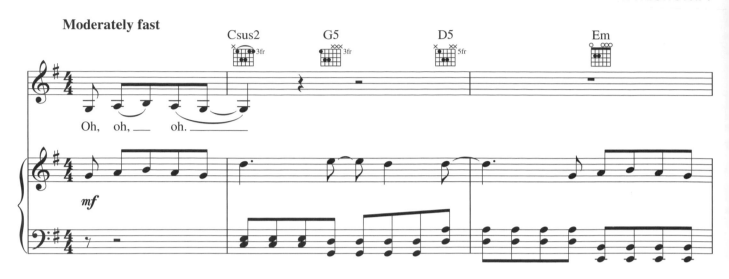

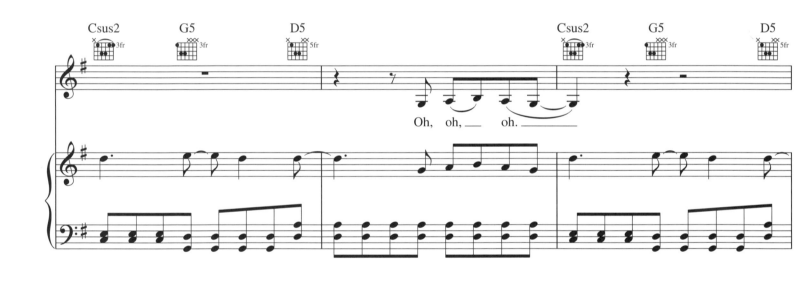

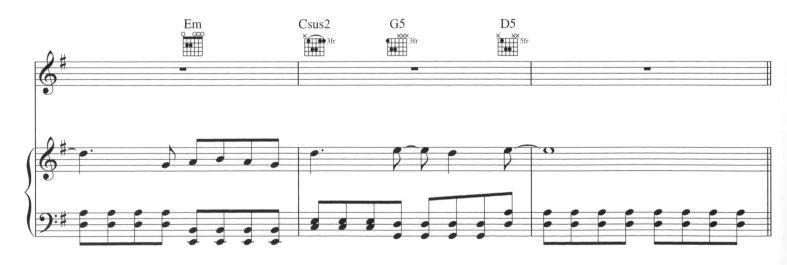

MY WISH

Words and Music by STEVE ROBSON
and JEFFREY STEELE

you.

May all

your dreams stay big.

Repeat and Fade

Optional Ending

RIVER OF LOVE

Words and Music by SHAWN CAMP,
BILLY BURNETTE and DENNIS MORGAN

Moderately fast

roll - in' on the riv-er of love.

{We'll Let's Let's} go roll - in' on the riv-er of love.

To Coda ⊕

1.

2.

OUR KIND OF LOVE

Words and Music by HILLARY SCOTT,
CHARLES KELLEY, DAVE HAYWOOD
and busbee

Male: You wear your smile like a
Male: Skip-pin' rocks and

sum-mer sky just shin-in' down on me and you.___
leav-in' foot-prints *Both:* down there on the riv-er - bank.___

And al-ways

THEN

Words and Music by ASHLEY GORLEY,
BRAD PAISLEY and CHRIS DUBOIS

Moderately

Lyrics:
I__ re-mem-ber try-in' not to stare the night_ that I first_
I__ re-mem-ber tak-in' you_ back to right_ where I first_

__ met you. You had me mes-mer-ized._ And
__ met you. You were so sur-prised._ There were

TODAY WAS A FAIRYTALE

Words and Music by
TAYLOR SWIFT

Time slows down when-ev-er you're a-

round. _____

But can you feel this mag-ic in the air? It must have been the

way you kissed me. _____ Fell in love when I saw you stand-in'

TWO IS BETTER THAN ONE

Words and Music by MARTIN JOHNSON
and TAYLOR SWIFT

Moderate Ballad

I re-mem-ber what you wore on the __ first day. __
I re-mem-ber ev-'ry look up-on __ your face, __

__ You came in-to my life, and I __ thought, hey, __ you know, __ this could __ be some-thing.
__ the way you roll your eyes, the way __ you taste. __ You make __ it hard __ for breath-ing.

'Cause ev-'ry-thing you do and words __ you say,
'Cause when I close my eyes and drift __ a-way,

YOU'RE LIKE COMIN' HOME

Words and Music by BRANDON KINNEY,
BRIAN MAHER and JEREMY STOVER

Rid - in' rest - less un - der bro -
Go a - head and let your hair

ken sky,
fall down.
wea - ry trav - 'ler, some - thin' miss - in' in - side, __ al - ways look -
This wan - der - lust, _____ it's __ gone now. __ Here in your

Recorded a half step lower.

WALK WITH YOU

Words and Music by MAIA SHARP
and EDWIN McCAIN

Gentle Ballad

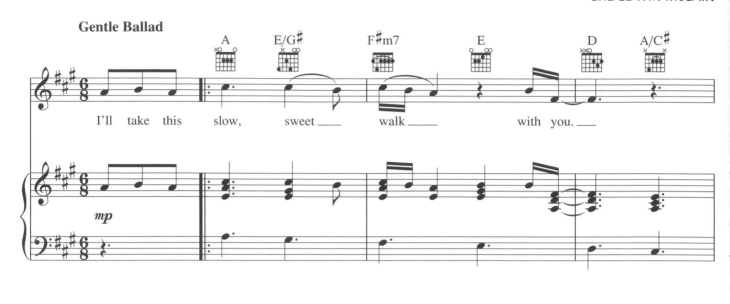

I'll take this slow, sweet ___ walk ___ with you. ___

You'll let ___ go of my ___ hand ___ to say, ___ "I

do." And he will dis-cov-er ___ just how

WHEN I LOOK AT YOU

Words and Music by JOHN SHANKS
and HILLARY LINDSEY

YOU RAISE ME UP

Words and Music by BRENDAN GRAHAM
and ROLF LOVLAND

seas.   I am   strong ____ when   I   am   on ____   your ____

shoul - ders. ____   You   raise   me   up   to   more   than   I ____   can   be.

The Most Romantic Music In The World

Arranged for piano, voice, and guitar

The Best Love Songs Ever - 2nd Edition

This revised edition includes 65 romantic favorites: Always • Beautiful in My Eyes • Can You Feel the Love Tonight • Endless Love • Have I Told You Lately • Misty • Something • Through the Years • Truly • When I Fall in Love • and more.

00359198 ....$19.95

The Big Book of Love Songs - 2nd Edition

80 romantic hits in many musical styles: Always on My Mind • Cherish • Fields of Gold • I Honestly Love You • I'll Be There • Isn't It Romantic? • Lady • My Heart Will Go On • Save the Best for Last • Truly • Wonderful Tonight • and more.

00310784 ....$19.95

The Christian Wedding Songbook

37 songs of love and commitment, including: Bonded Together • Cherish the Treasure • Flesh of My Flesh • Go There with You • Household of Faith • How Beautiful • I Will Be Here • Love Will Be Our Home • Make Us One • Parent's Prayer • This Is the Day • This Very Day • and more.

00310681 ....$16.95

The Bride's Guide to Wedding Music

This great guide is a complete resource for planning wedding music. It includes a thorough article on choosing music for a wedding ceremony, and 65 songs in many different styles to satisfy lots of different tastes. The songs are grouped by categories, including preludes, processionals, recessionals, traditional sacred songs, popular songs, country songs, contemporary Christian songs, Broadway numbers, and new age piano music.

00310615 ....$19.95

Broadway Love Songs

50 romantic favorites from shows such as *Phantom of the Opera, Guys and Dolls, Oklahoma!, South Pacific, Fiddler on the Roof* and more. Songs include: All I Ask of You • Bewitched • I've Grown Accustomed to Her Face • Love Changes Everything • So in Love • Sunrise, Sunset • Unexpected Song • We Kiss in a Shadow • and more.

00311558 ....$15.95

Country Love Songs - 4th Edition

This edition features 34 romantic country favorites: Amazed • Breathe • Could I Have This Dance • Forever and Ever, Amen • I Need You • The Keeper of the Stars • Love Can Build a Bridge • One Boy, One Girl • Stand by Me • This Kiss • Through the Years • Valentine • You Needed Me • more.

00311528 ....$14.95

The Definitive Love Collection - 2nd Edition

100 romantic favorites – all in one convenient collection! Includes: All I Ask of You • Can't Help Falling in Love • Endless Love • The Glory of Love • Have I Told You Lately • Heart and Soul • Lady in Red • Love Me Tender • My Romance • So in Love • Somewhere Out There • Unforgettable • Up Where We Belong • When I Fall in Love • and more!

00311681 ....$24.95

I Will Be Here

Over two dozen romantic selections from top contemporary Christian artists such as Susan Ashton, Avalon, Steven Curtis Chapman, Twila Paris, Sonicflood, and others. Songs include: Answered Prayer • Beautiful in My Eyes • Celebrate You • For Always • Give Me Forever (I Do) • Go There with You • How Beautiful • Love Will Be Our Home • and more.

00306472 ....$17.95

Love Songs

Budget Books Series

74 favorite love songs, including: And I Love Her • Cherish • Crazy • Endless Love • Fields of Gold • I Just Called to Say I Love You • I'll Be There • (You Make Me Feel Like) A Natural Woman • Wonderful Tonight • You Are So Beautiful • and more.

00310834 ....$12.95

The New Complete Wedding Songbook

41 of the most requested and beloved songs for romance and weddings: Anniversary Song • Ave Maria • Canon in D (Pachelbel) • Could I Have This Dance • Endless Love • I Love You Truly • Just the Way You Are • The Lord's Prayer • Through the Years • You Needed Me • Your Song • and more.

00309326 ....$12.95

New Ultimate Love and Wedding Songbook

This whopping songbook features 90 songs of devotion, including: The Anniversary Waltz • Can't Smile Without You • Could I Have This Dance • Endless Love • For All We Know • Forever and Ever, Amen • The Hawaiian Wedding Song • Here, There and Everywhere • I Only Have Eyes for You • Just the Way You Are • Longer • The Lord's Prayer • Love Me Tender • Misty • Somewhere • Sunrise, Sunset • Through the Years • Trumpet Voluntary • Your Song • and more.

00361445 ....$19.95

Romance - Boleros Favoritos

Features 48 Spanish and Latin American favorites: Aquello • Ojos Verdes • Bésame Mucho • El Reloj • Frenes • Inolvidable • La Vida Es Un Sueño • Perfidia • Siempre En Mi Corazón • Solamente Una Vez • more.

00310383 ....$16.95

Soulful Love Songs

Features 35 favorite romantic ballads, including: All My Life • Baby, Come to Me • Being with You • Endless Love • Hero • Just Called to Say I Love You • I'll Make Love to You • I'm Still in Love with You • Killing Me Softly with His Song • My Cherie Amour • My Eyes Adored You • Oh Girl • On the Wings of Love • Overjoyed • Tonight, I Celebrate My Love • Vision of Love • You Are the Sunshine of My Life • You've Made Me So Very Happy • and more.

00310922 ....$14.95

Selections from VH1's 100 Greatest Love Songs

Nearly 100 love songs chosen for their emotion. Includes: Always on My Mind • Baby, I Love Your Way • Careless Whisper • Endless Love • How Deep Is Your Love • I Got You Babe • If You Leave Me Now • Love Me Tender • My Heart Will Go On • Unchained Melody • You're Still the One • and dozens more.

00306506 ....$27.95